I got Sam by accident.  weeks. Little did I know that those 3 weeks would become 13 years and that it would be the best accident that ever happened to me.

I was home from college for winter break. My parents had lost their dog 6 months ago. It was the

first time I could ever remember our house being devoid of a dog. Yes, I had my cat and I loved her

but a cat is not the same as a dog. My sister brought her 2 dogs over to visit but they weren't my

dogs and they weren't there all the time. Even all the dogs that my family had had during my lifetime

hadn't really been mine. They had been either family dogs or my mother's dogs. It wasn't the same.I

I wanted a dog to call my own.

My mother received a call from the vet we had used for our previous dog. He had a puppy that

needed a foster. It had been injured and he thought it would recover better in a home than at the

hospital. He was looking to place the dog for 3 weeks while he found a permanent home for it. My

mother told me to go look at the dog and if I wanted to I could foster it for the time I was on winter

break.

I had a friend drive me to the vet's office. I went inside and was given the details of the puppy's background and medical needs before they brought the puppy out for me to meet. Turned out the puppy was more than injured. He had been abused and then tossed from a car. He had 3 broken ribs, a broken jaw, was severely malnourished, had 3 kinds of worms and understandably was terrified of people. He needed medication 4 times a day and would need to eat small meals 4 times a day. I was thinking about just saying no: this was going to be too much for me to handle. Then they brought him out and put him down on the floor.

He immediately ran and hid under the office chairs. This poor terrified puppy just crouched under the chairs and shook. I knew I had to give him a chance. I sat next to the chairs and talked to him for 2 hours. I didn't touch him or reach out to him. I just sat there and talked to him. Eventually he crawled out climbed into my lap and went to sleep. I sang rock a bye baby to him and stroked his head. He sighed gave my hand a lick and went on sleeping. Little did I know that in that moment he became mine and I became his. And it was that way for the next 13 years.

Those first 4 weeks were a real challenge. Sam as I named the puppy was terrified of everything

and everyone except me. He also had a tremendous amount of nervous energy. The house I was

living in with my parents was 3 stories. Sam would run up and down the stairs and throughout the

house until he exhausted himself and then come to me for affection. I introduced him to my cat and

they became best friends. They remained best friends forever. I introduced Sam to each person in

the family and all my friends. There were a few he liked, specifically my boyfriend (now my husband)

my mother and my grandfather. All others were tolerated.

I never believed in hitting an animal for misbehavior and knowing that Sam had been previously

abused I certainly wasn't going to hit him so I needed some way to punish him for misbehavior. He

hated to be apart from me so, go to your room become his punishment for misbehavior. It got to the

point that he knew when he had done something he would be punished for and after he did it he

would just walk past me and go into the bedroom and just stay there. His room was my room so his punishment really wasn't terrible. He had a comfy bed and chair in there to sleep on. It was where

he spent a good deal of time anyway. The only reason it was a punishment was that I wasn't there

with him and he knew I was mad at him.

    There was only 1 time that "go to your room" didn't completely work. Sam knew he wasn't

supposed to chase the cat. However this was a game that the 2 of them had invented and liked to

play. He would never hurt Mickey and she would never hurt him but they liked to chase each other

through the house. I didn't like this game. One day when they had been chasing each other for what

seemed like hours and I had told him at least 10 times to stop chasing the cat I had finally had

enough and told him " That's it . I've had it. Go to your room." He stopped chasing the cat looked at

me realized I was really annoyed with him and started up the stairs to our bedroom. Halfway up the

stairs he turned looked at me and started making noises somewhat between a growl and a whimper.

It reminded me of a kid protesting a punishment to a parent. I said, "Are you talking to me?" With

that he put his head down went up to the bedroom and stayed there until I told him he could come out. He didn't chase the cat the rest of the day but the next day they were back at it. Eventually I

realized that they both enjoyed this game and it had a set of rules they invented for themselves so I

stopped interfering.

Sam and Mickey slept together, played together and got into mischief together. One day after

work I came home to find ripped open boxes of cat yummies and dog yummies all over the floor. I

had 2 very happy very bloated animals sleeping together with yummies scattered around them. I

went into the kitchen and found the cabinet where I kept the yummies opened and a few things

knocked over. I don't KNOW but I suspect the scenario went something like this. They both wanted

treats. Nobody was home for them to beg from so they decided to take things into their own paws.

Mickey had no trouble jumping up on the counter so she could reach the cabinet. She then used her

claws to open the cabinet and pushed the boxes of treats onto the floor. Sam had no trouble ripping

the boxes open and dumping the treats out. The 2 of them then feasted. After that I got child proof locks for the cabinets.

Sam loved to run. When I would take him to Jim's house which had a big fenced in yard he would

run 10 times in a circle in one direction then turn and run 10 times in the other direction. He would

keep doing this switching directions every 10 circles until he had tired himself out. Then he would go

rest in the shade or tell me he was ready to come in the house. There was only 1 time this did not

occur. Jim had a large boxer who was fairly old when I got Sam. Spot was a gentle giant and

reacted to Sam as if Sam was his pup. He would share his food and his treats with Sam and would

cuddle with him to sleep. However Spot was older and did not run. He slowly walked around the

yard and then would lie under the grape vines and rest. One day we looked out the window at the 2

dogs and instead of seeing Sam running circles around the yard and Spot slowly walking around the

yard we saw both of them laying under the grape vines and Spot had his paw on Sam's back. First

we thought " oh how cute Spot's hugging Sam". Then we looked closer and realized Spot wasn't

hugging Sam, he was pining him down so he couldn't get up and run anymore.

Sam had occasional episodes when he would seem to not recognize where he was or what was

going on. He would bite anything or anyone that came near him. My vet after witnessing one such

episode diagnosed it as PTSD He said that after the abuse Sam had suffered before I got him he

would occasionally slip into memories of that time in his life and would just be trying to escape the

abuse. I learned that if I just sat away from him and gently spoke to him or sang Rock-a-Bye Baby

(our good night song) to him he would come out of the panic. After every episode like this he would

be completely exhausted and shaken. He would come and sit in my lap and pant and shake til he

calmed down and then went to sleep. Thankfully the longer I had him the less frequent these

episodes became and after a few years they stopped completely.

    The other shadow that persisted from his previous life was that Sam was totally defensive of me.

He only weighed 36 pounds at his heaviest but when it came to defending me from any perceived

danger he was.as my Uncle Lou used to say, 36 pounds of mean. Most of the time Sam was fine with anyone I had assured him was ok and to a select few he was even sweet and loving. However

nobody, even those he was normally affectionate with was allowed to do anything that he considered

a threat to me. His love, adoration and protection of me knew no bounds. He would have done

anything to keep me safe. I used to say he was both the protector and the protected because I felt

the same way. I had promised him that first day that nobody would ever hurt him again and I would

do everything in my power to make good on that promise.

    Sam's need to protect me gave him much more strength than you would expect from a 36 pound

dog. I always walked Sam on a chain link leash. This wasn't really necessary because he didn't pull

and never wanted to be out of my sight but that was his leash. We walked all over the neighborhood

and I never worried. One day as I was returning from a walk with him and it was just turning dark my

brother-in-law thought it would be funny to sneak up from behind me. Sam sensed someone behind

me and broke the metal leash, turned, knocked my brother-in-law to the ground and was going for his throat when I yelled his name and said its ok. As soon as I said that Sam got off of Marc came over

to me, wagged his tail and happily walked into the house with me. Needless to say Marc never tried

sneaking up on me again when I had Sam with me.

Sam went everywhere with me. When I was at college I had him living in the dorm with me and he

went to classes with me. When I finished college and we went back to live with my parents he was of

course with me there too. When I moved to my own apartment Sam was my rock and my protector.

One of my neighbors said to me that if I came home late at night he would worry about me and watch

for me out his window unless he knew I had Sam with me. He said he knew I was safe as long as

Sam was with me. Our life together was wonderful for 11 years. Then his abusive first 3 months

caught up with him and our time together became even more precious.

When Sam was 11 when during his regular annual exam the vet noticed something amiss in his

blood work. He ran more tests and found that Sam's kidneys weren't working the way they should be. He was put on a special diet in the hopes that the special diet would help. He didn't like it and I

would find all different ways to get him to eat the prescription food that he had to have. The diet

worked for awhile but the decline in his kidney function was inevitable. The vet said that he thought

that Sam's kidneys had been damaged from either the abuse or the malnutrition he had suffered as a

puppy. We kept him on the diet and also tried removing stress and keeping him from getting too hot

or tired or too cold. For a dog that always had a lot of energy it was strange when he started sleeping

a lot. He was still a happy playful dog and still wanted to be with me always but I could see it took a

lot out of him. I started staying home a lot so that he would be able to just be with me in the house

without putting out a lot of energy.

    The diet worked for about a year and then the kidneys got worse. We put him on a diet of chicken,

rice and cottage cheese. He couldn't have regular dog biscuits so I started making my own using

oatmeal and chicken broth which he was allowed. This worked for about another year. The vet kept

telling me that there was nothing that could be done; eventually the kidneys would just stop working.

Kidney disease doesn't get better; the best you can do is slow the progression which was what we

were doing.

　　I started researching anything I could find on treatment of kidney disease in dogs. My vet was

right; at the time there was no treatment available other than diet. I found one experimental treatment

that I considered. Then I found out that if I opted for this experimental treatment Sam would become

the property of the research facility. I decided that since he was afraid of most people and only felt

safe with me I could not do that to him. We continued the diet and kept him as happy and

comfortable as we could.

　　One day he wouldn't eat his chicken and rice or anything else. I took him in to the vet. After the

tests I was told "His kidneys aren't working at all. By all rights he should be dead. There is no kidney

function." I asked if he were in pain. The vet assured me Sam was not in pain; possibly

uncomfortable but not in pain. He then said to me ,"the only thing keeping him alive is his love for you. He doesn't want to leave you." I asked what we should do. He said I should let him eat

whatever he wanted to eat and we could try IV fluids 2x a day to keep him comfortable.

We did that. I would take him for his IV fluids in the morning before going to work. Then we would go

home and I'd make him comfortable and go to work. After work I'd take him back for another round of

IV treatment and after we would go home and he'd play with me and snuggle. Through it all he was

happy and playful and loving. He slept with me every night as he had always done. We went for

short walks which he enjoyed and car rides which he had always loved. He would eat cooked beef if I

hand fed him and potato chips so that would be what he got for breakfast and dinner. Throughout it

all he was my protector, my love and my life. One day at the vet appointment after tests the vet again

said to me " He is only alive because he won't leave you"

    That night he wouldn't eat. I tried hand feeding him but he wouldn't take any meat or chips. I

thought ok we'll try later. He tried to curl up with me to sleep but he couldn't get comfortable. I tried taking him for a walk. He fell down after a few steps. I carried him to the couch and sat down with

him. He put his head on my lap and tried to sleep but again couldn't get comfortable. I took his head

in my hands and kissed him. I told him "Sam I love you and I don't want to lose you but if you're in

this much pain or discomfort I would rather you were dead". I swear on some level he understood

me. He gave my face a kiss, put his head in my lap and went sleep. He never woke up. When I

realized he was gone, I told him I would see him again someday and that for now he should look for

Grandpop Sam when he got to heaven. I knew my grandfather had loved Sam and Sam had loved

my grandfather. I knew Sam would be safe and happy til I got to be with him again.

Clemens

Clemens was really more my husband's dog than mine. She came into our lives at a time

when I just couldn't fully give my heart to her and she needed someone to do exactly that. We had lost our first dog Sam a few weeks before Clemens showed up and I wasn't ready to open my heart to

another dog just yet.

For weeks after losing Sam I kept imagining I saw him. When I was driving I'd see him on the

sidewalks I was passing. When I walked anyplace I would see him being walked by someone else.

Somehow although the vet had told me Sam had passed away I couldn't accept that and instead

imagined him everywhere. I dreamed about him lost and crying for me and being unable to get to

him. Then one day Clemens showed up at our house. She was the spitting image of Sam except for

being slightly smaller and of course female not male. She was skinny, scared, dirty and matted. I

started feeding her. I was hoping to get close enough to her to see if she had a tag that I could use to

trace back to her owners and get her back to them.

Jim (my husband) kept telling me about the mangy looking dog that was hanging around. He kept

admonishing me to not feed it. He didn't want it hanging around and kept saying if we don't feed it

perhaps it will just leave and go home. I kept sneaking food out to her and trying to gain her trust.

Jim's mother who lived with us kept sneaking food to her as well. The dog stuck around. After a few

days she let me get close enough to see she had no collar or ID of any kind just a piece of string

around her neck. I didn't want to keep her I just wanted to find her a safe place to be. My constant

words were " I don't ever want another dog. No dog can replace Sam." It took a long time for me to

come to terms with Sam's death and realize that getting another dog is not replacing the one before.

Rather it is honoring their memory by giving another dog and yourself the joy of the loving bond

between dog and person.

    One day about a week after the dog showed up Jim was doing some body work on our car. He

was working in the driveway and had sandpaper, paint and body filler out there. He came in the

house to get something and when he went back out his sandpaper was gone. He came back into the

house yelling that the "damn dog took my sandpaper". For some reason, that I still haven't figured

out 40 years later, that was the point at which he decided that the dog could stay until we found the owners or a home for her. He brought her into the enclosed porch we had in the backyard and set

her up with dishes and a pillow to sleep on.

    I spent the next week feeding her, taking her out of the enclosure to do her business and getting

her used to being handled and making and putting up signs trying to find her owners. I ran ads in the

paper. I took her to the vet to get her medically cleared. This was all done after work. I was still

grieving my Sam and did not want to keep this dog. That was when everything came crashing down.

    My mother- in -law told me that my Sam had died because I didn't take care of him. (my vet had

said that nobody could have taken better care of him), my husband did not defend me and in fact told

me that I should be more understanding of his mother. Then he decided to tell me all the things I was

doing wrong about trying to find this lost dog's owner and caring for her. In addition he told me how I

wasn't doing enough for him or his mother. I was working full time taking care of the house and going

to school. He was not working or going to school and was focusing on his writing as he wanted to be a writer. Anyway it was too much for me and I walked out. I went to see my parents and thought

about leaving him. I was gone for about a week. Friends that knew us both kept calling me and

telling me how miserable he was without me so I went back.

When I got back everything had changed about the dog's situation. Jim had decided we were

keeping her. He had brought her into the house and she was now our dog. According to him what

happened was… He had been keeping her in the back yard enclosure but then it started raining and

the water came into the enclosure. He saw that the dog was sleeping on top of the furniture we had

out there so she could stay dry. He brought her into our finished basement to keep her warm and dry

but then decided that she was lonely down there by herself so after making sure that she got along

with his mother's dog he gave her free rein of the house and named her Clemens. I was told to stop

looking for her owners or a new home. He said she was now our dog but in reality she was his dog. I

just didn't have it in me fo love another dog. It took me a few years to open my heart to her.

Of all the dogs I've had over the years Clemens was the most grateful and the easiest. Unlike my

other dogs that could be very finicky about what they ate Clemens was just happy to have a full food

dish. She wasn't particular about what was in the dish as long as it was something edible that would

fill her belly. She was thrilled to sleep in bed with us but she was satisfied with the couch or a blanket

and pillow on the floor next to the bed. Unlike some dogs that don't come immediately when they are

called Clemens came immediately no matter what she was in the middle of. I think she was so glad

to have a home and people to take care of her she didn't want to take any chances that we might not

wait for her.

Clemens got along great with Jim's mother's dog Hassenpheffer. They became great friends and

would eat, sleep and play together. They shared everything. Except when Hassenpheffer would

decide to do something bad like steal food from off the table. Clemens would never join in any

activities that might get her in trouble. When Hass decided to do something that would get them in

trouble whether digging in the yard, stealing food or chewing on things other than their toys Clemens would walk away and go rest on the bed. She was very well behaved and a little lady.

Clemens adored Jim. It was as if she recognized that he was the one that gave her a home. She

followed him around like a little shadow. Although I fed her and took care of her he was her person.

It made total sense. I was not yet ready to love another dog.

We had Clemens for about 2 years when my mother-in-law's dog Hass passed away. She decided

that she wanted another dog right away. I was sent out looking for a dog for her. I was given

instructions to get a dog that looked just like Hass. My mother-in-law had decided that since after

Sam died Clemens had showed up and looked just like him a dog would show up that would look just

like Hass. I went to several shelters and never found a dog that looked like Hass but did bring home

a new dog for her. She instantly decided that she didn't want him and decided to make Clemens her

dog.

Jim was not happy with this arrangement and neither was Clemens. Jim accepted it because it was his mother and he wanted her to have the company of a dog. Besides the new puppy Buster

was one of those dogs that you can't help but fall in love with. Clemens accepted it because that was

her nature. She was totally accepting of her fate whatever that was and truly happy and grateful to

just have a steady supply of food, affection and a warm, safe place to sleep. Jim's mother deciding to

take her did not interfere with any of these things for Clemens. She had Jim's attention and affection

during the day as well as that of Jim's mother. I made sure she had her 2 meals every day while they

provided snacks. The only difference was that Clemens had slept with me and Jim every night and

now Jim's mother took Clemens into her bedroom at night and closed the door. Clemens had to

sleep with her instead of us- or should I say instead of her favorite person Jim. She was still sleeping

in a warm comfortable bed with a loving person. As soon as Jim's mother opened the bedroom door

in the morning. Clemens would run into our room and snuggle in next to her person-Jim.

    Clemens was so good with the puppy. We worried at first that his puppy antics might annoy her.

They didn't. Rather she seemed to enjoy playing with him although she did from the start let him

know that she was the boss. It turned out to be a good thing that she established this while he was a

baby because by the time he was full grown he outweighed her by 90 pounds. It didn't matter; she

was still the boss.

When Clemens was about 8 years old she developed glaucoma. She needed drops put in her

eyes twice a day. In all my years of having dogs I have never had a dog before or after her that was

so cooperative about getting drops. She would come over when I showed her the bottle and sit next

to me. She was totally cooperative with me holding her eyes open and putting the drops in. I don't

think I myself would be so compliant. It was almost as if she understood that the drops were to help

her. Of course after each treatment Jim would hug her and snuggle her and tell her what a good girl

she was so I guess that helped.

After a few years the drops stopped working and unfortunately Clemens went blind. You might

think that she would be depressed or stop doing things or even like most people refuse to do things and just feel sorry for herself and act helpless. Not Clemens (and as I've since learned not most

animals). She learned to navigate around the house by following the walls. She already knew the

location of all the furniture so that wasn't a problem. She had no trouble finding her way around the

house, to the back door, to her dishes and to her and our beds. She did have some trouble when she

was out in the backyard but Buster became her seeing eye companion in the yard. He kept an eye

on her and stopped her if she was going to walk into anything. The only time she had trouble was if

we moved the furniture or left something on the floor that didn't belong there. We learned to be more

careful with our things.

    Clemens had a wonderful life and loved being pampered, loved and cared for. She showed her

appreciation every day. One day I took her out, gave her breakfast and her kisses and told her to go

back to sleep with Jim. She was old at that point and had started to sleep much of the day. When I

got home from work I found her in the bed snuggled in her blanket, with her head on the pillow. She

had passed during the day content in her bed.

Buster

I had been through the shelter twice. I hadn't found what I was looking for. I was supposed to be

getting a dog for my mother-in-law. She had recently lost her fox terrier and wanted another fox

terrier. I was to get her a female fox terrier that was white with brown spots and full grown it shouldn't

be more than 30 pounds. I hadn't found anything like that at the shelter. Then something caught my

eye. There was an adorable 12 week old puppy in the cage next to where I was standing. He was

putting his nose and paws through the bars of the cage and trying to reach me. When he saw me

looking at him he started running around the cage, stepping on his brother's head, getting his brother

to fight and generally putting on quite the show. He was adorable. I knew he wasn't what I was there

to get but I asked to see him anyway.

When the attendant handed him to me I couldn't believe how calm and gentle he was in my arms.

I put him on my shoulder and he gave my ear a lick and settled down for a nap. I knew I couldn't take

him but I had to ask about him anyway. The attendants told me he was a fox terrier mix and would

get no bigger than 30 pounds. I had found the dog I would take home for my mother- in -law.

   I carried him around with me and went to fill out the papers. As I started to fill them out I started

thinking how sad his brother would be left there at the shelter in a cage all by himself. I couldn't do

that to him. I started walking back to the attendant to ask about the other puppy. I got there just as a

man was telling the attendant he wanted to adopt the puppy he had in his arms. It was my puppie's

brother. Now that I knew the other puppy would have a home too I felt better about taking this one. I

went and filled out the paperwork and waited while they called my references and called home to

make sure the other adults in the home were ok with me bringing home a puppy. Once I was

approved I was told to go to another building to get the supplies I would need. It was cold so I put the

puppy inside my coat with just his little nose peeking out. He was happy to be just carried around this

way.

The ride home was a bit of an adventure. I had brought a laundry basket with a blanket in it to put

the puppy in. We got to the car and I gently placed the puppy in the laundry basket in the back seat

of the car. I covered him with the blanket because I was worried that even with the heat on he might

get a chill. The drive home started out smoothly. The puppy was asleep in the basket. However

after about 5 minutes he woke up. He didn't cry or whimper but he did crawl out from the blanket, tip

the basket over on its side ,crawl under the seat, climb up onto the front seat and squirm his way into

my lap. I had to drive home with the puppy on my lap the whole way. He never made a sound just

went to sleep on my lap.

On the way home I stopped where my husband was working so he could meet the new puppy. My

husband took one look at the puppy and said, "there's no way he's a fox terrier. He's a German

shepherd. And there's no way he's only going to be 30 pounds look at the size of his paws." I said

"Do you want me to take him back?" Knowing full well that there was no way this puppy was going back; as far as I was concerned he was mine. Yes I had gotten him for my mother-in-law but he was

going to live with me. She lived with us so it wasn't an issue. My husband said no you brought him

home we'll keep him. Hopefully mom will like him.

My mother-in-law did not like him. She didn't want him. She said she didn't want a male, and he

didn't look like the dog she had lost, and he wasn't a fox terrier like she wanted. The paperwork I had

been given by the shelter listed him as a fox terrier but my mother in law didn't care. She relented a

little and gave him the name Buster Brown which was shortened to Buster.

We tried having him be her dog. It didn't work. She kept calling our dog Clemens into her room

and closing the door; therefore keeping Clemens in with her and leaving the puppy Buster all alone.

After this happened consistently for a few days we decided Buster would become ours and he did.

Clemens was ours too and while she didn't mind being in the bedroom with my mother-in-law as soon

as the door opened she would run out of the room to be with us. That was fine. We had 2 dogs.

Buster the baby and Clemens the dog n charge.

    Watching Clemens and Buster interact was really funny. He was a baby and therefore let her take

charge. She was great. They slept together when they were with us and when it was just the 2 of

them. They played together and shared their toys. When he got too rough in his play she gave hm a

little nip to remind him who was boss. As he got bigger; eventually he weighed 3 times what she did,

he still deferred to her.

    From the time I brought him home buster was the consumate Southern Gentleman. He was the

easiest dog I ever had to house train. He had 1 accident in the house the first night I brought him

home. I caught him peeing in the house, picked him up brought him outside where he finished told

him he was a good boy and that was the last time he ever peed or pooped in the house. He never

stole food or anything else. He would sometimes see something he wanted such as a ball that wasn't

his and bring it to us to ask if he could have it. If I said "no that's not yours" he would put it down and go get one of his toys. If I said,"yes you can have that" he would happily pick it back up and trot off

with it. He never begged for food but he knew when he was supposed to eat both breakfast and

dinner. I never needed an alarm clock. My normal routine was to get up at 6am give the 2 dogs

breakfast, take them out and then start getting ready for work. At exactly 6am every morning he

would sit next to my side of the bed and stare at me. Somehow his staring always woke me up.

The dogs got dinner at 6pm. The same thing would happen. Whatever I was doing and wherever I

was in the house at exactly 6pm Buster would come find me and stare at me. He would stare until I

acknowledged that it was dinner time and I stopped what I was doing and got the dogs their dinner.

    Buster grew to be a large dog. At his prime he weighed 110 pounds. If he wasn't so gentle he

could easily hurt someone accidentally. Thankfully he was by nature a gentle giant and I taught him

the word gentle so that when necessary he would be extra careful. He liked to comfort other dogs

and especially puppies when we were in the waiting room at the vet's office. He would go over to any dog that was anxious and if I got permission from the dog's owner he would snuggle the other dog,

kiss it and sometimes take his paw and pet the other dog. If the other dog was very small or a puppy

I would say to him "gentle" and he would very gently put his paw on the other dog and look at me

before petting the other dog. He would also do the same to comfort kittens that were anxious and

cats too unless they started to mew. For some reason the sound of mewing spooked him and if a cat

mewed he'd back away from them and try to hide behind me. It was quite comical seeing this large

dog trying to crawl away and hide from a cat that was less than a 10th of his size. I could never figure

out what it was about the mewing of the cat that bothered him but he loved both kittens and cats

unless the cat mewed. Thankfully, even when he was spooked he never tried to hurt them.

    Buster knew instinctively when he needed to be extra careful around someone. He would jump up

on me every time I came in the door and he would get in my way whenever I was walking anywhere.

Not so with anyone that was elderly, ill or weak. For those people he never jumped up on them and always got out of their way. He would pull me every time I tried to walk him on the leash but if my

mother or elderly aunt was the one holding the leash he walked like a perfect gentleman without

pulling at all.

    Buster was a dog that truly saw his mission in life to be making his mommy and daddy happy. If

he did something wrong and you used the word no or bad he reacted as if he had been beat. This

dog who had never been hit in his life reacted like he was beat at the sound of the word "bad". I

made sure to use that word as infrequently as possible. There were 2 times that I used that word and

I felt terrible about it. Once as a puppy he put his feet on the stove. I said "NO BAD DOG'"in the

most authoritative voice I could muster. I felt bad cause I knew he would be upset but I wanted to

make sure that he never put his feet on the stove when it was on. The other time was when he found

a plastic bag and started playing with it and putting his head in it. I didn't want him to accidentally get

his head stuck and suffocate so I used those words again. Poor Buster was so upset both times that

he curled up in the corner and cried himself to sleep.

As gentle, loving and well behaved as Buster was he also was very protective of both me and my husband. We had a gazebo in the yard. I liked to sit out there sometimes. Buster would never come into the gazebo but would lie across the doorway. Nobody was allowed to come into the gazebo while I was in there unless I said "Buster let them in". Then he would move out of the doorway. If I did not say that Buster would just stand in the doorway between me and the person and stare them down. You could almost hear him thinking "If you want to get to my Mommy you have to go through me first." He had his own ideas about protection sometimes. Once my husband was putting new windows in our basement. He was sitting on the ground with his back to the street. Buster saw my husband with his back to the street while people were passing by. He must have decided this wasn't safe because he ran out of the house (which he knew he wasn't allowed to do), ran off the porch and ran to where my husband was sitting, checked that all was safe and then sat with his back to my husbands back so that he could observe all that was on the street. He even guarded my husband's tools while he went inside to get a tool he had forgotten.

When his doggy sister Clemens went blind Buster became her seeing eye dog until she learned to

navigate the house and the yard by herself. Buster would lead her through the house to her dish. He

would lead her to the back door to go out and down the back steps. While they were outside he

would lead her around the yard and make sure she didn't bump into any obstacles. He did the same

in the house. Once she became able to navigate by herself he stopped leading her but still kept a

protective eye on her so that he could help if there was an obstacle in her way.

We had this wonderful dog for almost 15 years. When he was a few months short of his 15th

birthday he developed the dog equivalent of Lou Gehig's disease. His muscles were atrophying and

he was losing the ability to walk by himself. The vet said physical therapy might help slow the

progression of the disease. I started doing a series of exercises with him several times a day. I

would move his paws and help him walk using a splint. I would move him from side to side and

manipulate his legs and paws. He was a trooper throughout all the exercise routines and never complained or refused to let me work on him. After awhile, his vet suggested that he might do better

with some exercises that required him to be at the veterinary hospital. I brought him in one day and

left him so that he could have his therapy session. He tried so hard. Buster and the vet were good

friends. This vet had been his doctor for his entire life. The session went very well and he looked

great when I brought him home that night. The next day I took him for another session. The vet

worked with him and then felt that he might be able to walk with the use of the sling. The vet tech

held buster up with the sling while the vet called him to come. Buster tried so hard to please the vet

that he had a heart attack from the strain. That was the end of my Southern Gentleman.

                                                                    Mackintosh

Mackintosh, Mackintosh, mommy's little Mackintosh"

"Mackintosh, Mackintosh, mommy loves her Mackintosh"

My voice echoed off the walls of the vet's examining room. My tears fell on my sweet baby boy.

He lifted his head and with great effort pulled himself an inch or so closer so his head was in my lap.

I scratched his head and ears and thought to myself". He has to get better, he has to recover. What

would I do without my sweet little Mackintosh. My little shadow."

I had gotten Mack when he was just 5 weeks old. His mother had rejected him and refused to

feed him so the shelter had been bottle feeding him. I had waited 6 months after losing my previous

dog before realizing I needed to have a dog in my life. This is how I wound up at the shelter on this

day. I had looked at all the dogs and puppies in all the cages and hadn't found "the one". You know

what I mean. The one that you look at and say" this is my dog". I was about to leave when I felt a

tiny tongue on my arm. I turned and looked. I saw this tiny puppy in the cage just looking at me. I told the kennel attendant "I want to see this one". She proceeded to tell me I didn't. She explained

that he was a bitter. She showed me all the band-aids on her fingers from the times she had put food

or water in his cage. I insisted. She called over another kennel attendant, whose fingers also were

covered in band-aids. This one too told me I didn't want to see that puppy because he bit everyone.

I insisted and they relented with the warning that if I got bit don't say they didn't warn me. He

snuggled my neck, licked my ear peed on me, and went to sleep. The attendants were in shock that

he didn't bite me. They made me give him back so they could clean him up. And gave me towels to

dry myself off. I said I wanted him and they directed me to where I had to go to fill out the paperwork.

I insisted they give him back to me while I filled out the papers and went through the procedures. I

carried him around with me. He slept on my shoulder while I filled out the paperwork and waited for

the shelter to check my credentials. They were hesitant about letting me adopt him because he was

a border collie puppy which are thought to be difficult to train. They were afraid I might abuse him if I

got frustrated with his stubborness. They called the vet I had used for all my previous dogs. When they heard from him that the only thing bad that might happen to the dog if they allowed me to have

him was "He will be spoiled rotten" they allowed me to adopt him.

He did prove to be a challenge. I loved him dearly and he was a wonderful dog even as a

stubborn, willful puppy. The problem was he had sooooo much energy and was very intelligent so he

was easily bored. At one point,, after being told by numerous people that the problem was that he

was meant to be a working dog and I was depriving him by not giving him any sheep to herd or job to

do I actually considered giving him away. I went with him to my vet and asked his advice. His

answer was" You love him right? And he obviously loves you. That's all that matters. He'll be fine.".

At that point I realized I could never give him up but I could find jobs for him around the house. Thus

began my search for things that would exercise his body and engage his brain.

The first thing I tried were the puzzle toys they make for dogs. I must of bought at least 5 of them of various types. He was too smart for all of them. All those ads saying they would keep the dog

engaged for hours might have been true for other dogs but Mac had them figured out and the treat

inside eaten within 5 minutes. Obviously, I needed something more challenging. The idea that

occurred to me was actually his idea.

    Mac loved to carry things around and bring them to different places. He also loved watching

things I did and wanted to be with me always. And so began our laundry day game. Every time I did

laundry I would take a big laundry bag and put all the dirty cloths in the bag and tie it shut. Mac would

then drag the bag to the top of the stairs and push the bag to the bottom of the stairs. He always

acted so pleased with himself when he did this. After the 1st few times he would come running as

soon as he saw or heard me get the laundry bag out of the drawer..

    The next game we designed was also by his design. Make started his life with us with about 5

toys. He slowly acquired 33. He learned the names of all of them and would go get whichever one you asked him to get. So we started out with me just asking for specific toys and then he would

search around the floor looking for the right one and then bringing it to me. That developed into me

hiding a toy and then asking for it. This meant he had to look a little harder. The 3rd game took

advantage of the border collie obsessive-compulsive nature. Every night before he went to sleep with

me Mac had to line up all his toys in a specific order. When it was 5 toys or when it got to 30 there

was always a specific order that they toys went in. When I got up in the morning I would sometimes

switch the order of a few of them. He would come out of the bedroom look at the line up of his toys

and realize something was wrong. He would then replace them in the order that they had been in. If

I removed a toy or toys from the line-up completely he would search the house til he found the

missing toy and put it in the line-up where it belonged. Then he would give a satisfied sigh and go eat

his breakfast.

    Mac had inside toys and outside toys. I didn't allow him to bring inside toys outside or outside toys

inside. He did sometimes try to sneak them from inside to outside or vice versa but a simple reminder of where it belonged was enough to get him to leave it where it belonged. When were were

outside he would take all his toys out of the gazebo where we kept them and we would play with them

together. When it was time to go inside originally I would have to go around the yard and pick them

all up and put them away. One day he started helping me by picking them up and following me into

the gazebo. This turned into another job for him. At the end of our time outside I would just tell him

put your toys away and he would gather up the toys one by one and put them in the gazebo. When

all of them had been put away he would go to the back steps and wait to go in with me.

    Mac was my little shadow. From the day I brought him home he followed me wherever I went. I

couldn't even go to the bathroom or take a shower without him following me. If I closed the door he

would lay outside the bathroom door. I was never sure if this was his way of protecting me or if he

just didn't like me out of his sight. When he was a baby he loved to run around our fenced in yard but

again didn't like me out of his sight. Soooo he would run around the yard and then run back to me, make sure I was still out there with him and then go back to running around the yard. As he got older I

guess he was more confident that I wasn't going anywhere and he would check back less often. Now

don't get the impression that him being my little shadow meant that he would come in the house when

I told him to. If I called him into the house and he wasn't ready to go in he would either completely

ignore me or more often come running to me and then a foot or so away from the door turn and run

the other way. He could keep this game up for hours. I couldn't. I eventually learned that the words"

Mommy's going to get the hose." would get him in the house immediately. He hated getting wet.

    Mac loved to play chase. We would go in the yard at opposite corners. I would yell go and he

would start chasing me. The aim was to touch me with his nose. Once he touched me with his nose

we would reverse and I would chase him until I touched his tushie with my hand. Guess who spent

most of their time as the one being chased. In typical border collie fashion he was fast and nimble.

Most of the time as I was about to touch him he would dodge my outstretched hand and dart away.

As much as Mac loved to play chase with me he loved to play chase with all creatures. He would

chase any cats or squirrels that came into the yard. He would never hurt them and if they stayed still

he ignored them. For him it was just the thrill of the chase. Rodents except squirrels were a different

matter. He would kill them with a quick grab of the neck, a swing to the right, a swing to the left and

then he'd bring the dead creature to me very proud of himself.

Mac being a typical border collie would also make up some games himself that weren't fun for me.

He was very intelligent and had an incredible vocabulary. He liked to hide things and then wait for me

to ask him for them. One morning when I was getting ready for work I couldn't find my car keys. I

was running around the house looking for them. I knew I always kept them in the same place so I

was getting more and more frustrated. My husband as a joke said I should ask the dog. I stopped

and said "Mac where are mommy's keys?" He looked at me ran to the couch and looked under it and

ran back to me. I then said " Mac get mommy's keys". He ran to the couch and pulled my keys from

under it. I then had to say "Mac bring mommy her keys". Which he proceeded to do but would not let me have them until I said "Mac give mommy her keys". I was late for work because of this but

thankfully my boss had a border collie herself so when I explained why I was late she just nodded and

laughed. Good thing I had an understanding boss. From then on whenever I couldn't find something

I would ask Mac. And I started putting my keys in places that he couldn't reach.

Unlike most dogs Mack was not afraid of thunder and lightning or fireworks. He loved both. When

it was thundering and lightning he would insist that I sit outside with him on our porch and watch the

lightning. On the 4th of July he would sit outside with me or on the porch with me to watch the

fireworks. He would nudge my head in the direction of whatever fireworks he wanted me to look at.

He was also thrilled with holiday lights. During the month of December as people started decorating

the outside of their house with Christmas lights and decorations his nightly walks became longer and

longer as more and more decorations.went up. He had to stop and admire the decorations at each

house. He was particularly amused by an animated jack in the box on one neighbor's lawn. He would stop and watch for the jack in the box to come out. When it did he would bark do his little

happy dance watch it go back down and then sit and wait for it again.

    I thought back to last Christmas. For years friends that had kids had told me how they would take

their kids to the christmas light display at Jones Beach. They would express how much the kids

enjoyed it and exciting they found it. I always envied them being able to see the display through the

eyes of their kids. I had decided if they could take their kids to the display I could take Mac. So I put

him in the car and off we went. On the drive over to jones beach he was thrilled at all the decorated

houses we passed. He wagged his tail, made his happy sounds and did his happy dance.

    We got to the Christmas display and he could not control his enthusiasm. He ran from one place

in the car to another. Wagging, barking and doing his happy dance. When he saw something that

had him particularly thrilled he pushed my head in the direction of the display. It brought back to me

all the joy I felt as a child at Christmas time. I was so glad I had done this with him and given him this joyful experience

I looked down at the sweet little head on my lap. I stopped singing and sighed. How could I live

without this sweet little shadow. We had been through so much together. When the vet first told me

that Mac had had a stroke and was paralyzed from the neck down I had told him "I don't care, just get

him well enough to go home and I'll carry him all over.". Dr. Alan had looked at me with a sad smile

and said" I know you'd be willing and would do everything possible to keep him comfortable but he

would be miserable. This is an active playful dog. He wants to run and jump and play. He would be

so unhappy not being able to get around by himself. Think about what's best for him." Dr. Alan said

that I didn't need to make a decision right away. We would give it a week and see if any of the

treatments they were doing helped him recover any movement. Today was day 6.

I started crying again. My tears fell on Mac's head and woke him. He gave a little cry and

managed to lick my hand. I shushed him and told him everything would be ok. I remembered all the

times before I had told him that and it had been true. He signed and went back to sleep. I smiled

through my tears thinking about all the fun times we had.

Mac had never walked well on the leash. My fault I know. I had never taught him good leash

manners. We had a big fenced in yard so I never felt the need to walk him. So when I did

occasionally walk him he pulled like a crazy and I had to struggle to stay on my feet and not get

dragged. That all changed when he tore the ligaments in his knee. After the surgery to repair the

knee he wasn't allowed to go in the yard to play. He was only allowed to walk on the leash in the

yard to do his business and come back in. I had to do this for the 1st week and then gradually every

week increase slightly the amount he walked on the leash. First we were to stay in the yard and then

on the sidewalk for short distances. Starting just 1 house away and gradually increasing to all the way around the block. Thus at the age of 5 Mac finally learned leash manners. Once we had gotten

to the goal of all the way around the block the vet said all was well and the knee was fine. However,

because there had been an injury Mac needed to exercise by walking every day twice a day. So for

the next 10 years every day morning and late afternoon we walked around the neighborhood. I got to

meet many of my neighbors this way and Mac made many friends along the way.

    My mind came back to the present. Today was day 6. Tomorrow I would have to make the

decision on whether to keep Mac alive but paralyzed or let him go. I knew Dr. Alan was right that Mac

would be unhappy unable to play or run or even eat by himself. He had been miserable after his

knee surgery when he just had to be kept inactive. How would he deal with not being able to do

anything by himself. But…… he had been a huge part of my life for 15 years. He was my constant

companion. He had shared my life, my heart and yes my bed. How would I manage without him?

The vet's office had closed hours ago. Dr. Alan was staying so I could have more time with my Mac.

I realized it was getting late. I told the doctor I would be going and he could take Mac back to his

kennel. I kissed Mac's head and told him". "You sleep. Mommy will be back in the morning." Then I

covered him with his favorite blanket and handed him to Dr. Alan. Mac slept through it, just waking up

enough to kiss me as I handed him to the doctor.

    I went home with a heavy heart. I spent a restless night and was up pacing around the house

most of the night. It was around 8am; the vet's office opened at 9. I knew I would have to make my

decision by then. At 8;45 the phone rang. It was Dr. Alan. He told me he was making his morning

rounds and found Mac dead ,covered in his favorite blanket with the stuffed animal I had left with him

(the one he had slept with for many years) under his chin. I went to the vet's office so I could say a

final good-bye to Mac. I sat with him, talked to him and hugged and kissed him. And I thought to

myself" this sweet wonderful dog had even at the end taken care of me. He saved me from having to

make a horrible decision. I whispered, "Than you Mackintosh for this and for the 15 years you shared your life with me. Mommy loves you and will always love you." Then I went home, lit a white candle

and sent Mack's spirit to join my grandfather who I knew would take care of him in Heaven until I

could join him someday.

Baby

I had lost my sweet Mackintosh 2 weeks before. I didn't think I was ready for another dog yet.

Then my husband and I returned home from an evening out and realized there was no wagging,

barking, loving presence waiting to greet us as we walked in the door. We looked at each other and

both said"its time for another dog". The next day when I went to the shelter where I volunteered I told

the staff that I was looking to adopt a dog. They knew I had just lost Mackintosh. and were very

supportive and understanding. They had me list the dogs that I worked with as a volunteer and

decide if any of then would be the right fit. They asked me what I was looking for. I told them that I wanted a dog not a puppy and someone that wasn't too large for me to handle but wasn't a small dog

either. Most of all I wanted a dog that would think that I was the most important thing in the world just

like my previous dogs had. Funny thing, is though I didn't realize it at the time, any dog that is loved

and cared for by someone will think that. I didn't care what kind or the age (though my husband did

care about the age) I just cared that it was healthy and loving.

    I looked at about 12 dogs and met with each of them but none seemed to decide they were mine.

Yes, I believed then and still do that a dog decides if they want you as much as you decide if you want

them. There was only one that was a possibility but when I tried walking her I realized she was too

large and powerful for me to walk. Thankfully she was adopted by someone else the next day. I was

ready to give up for awhile and just wait til the right dog showed up when Nancy the adoption advisor

said to me, " We have a dog that I think would be perfect for you." She told me the dog's name and I

said that I hadn't considered her because she seemed totally wild and out of control in her kennel. In

fact they had to put padding on all sides of her kennel because she would jump and run so much that she would hit herself on the bars. I had never even tried walking her because she was so crazy.

Nancy told me that once she was out of the kennel she didn't act like that. I agreed to meet her. I sat

on the floor of the meet and greet room and my husband sat in a chair in the room. Nancy brought

the dog into the room. The dog looked around the room saw me walked over and gave me a kiss.

Then she curled up in my lap and went to sleep. I had been chosen. We filled out the paperwork

renamed her Baby and gave her back to Nancy to go back to her kennel with the promise to Baby

that we would be there the next day to take her home. I hated sending her back to her kennel; she

looked so sad. But my car was unreliable that day and I didn't want to take a chance of getting stuck

with a dog that didn't know me.

    We were back bright and early the next day. After again going through all the information they

had on Baby they got her from her kennel and handed us the leash. Baby had been with them for 6

months and until she was presented to us nobody had even inquired about her. All visitors to the shelter had, like me, seen her acting crazy in her kennel and rejected her as too wild. Her former

owners had given her to the shelter because she tended to try to dig under the fence in their yard or

jump over it. We were warned not to leave her in the yard by herself. That was not a problem for me.

In my 50 years of dog parenting I had never left a dog in the yard by themselves. My attitude was

and is if I wouldn't leave a 3 year old in the yard alone I wouldn't leave a dog in the yard alone.

Anyway, I walked her out of the shelter and the staff asked me if I wanted them to help me get her

into my car. I was about to say yes, thinking that she might balk at getting into a strange car with a

strange person. She surprised us all. She ran to the car with me in tow sat at the back door and as

soon as I opened the door she jumped in. My husband got in I got in and off we went.

I expected her to be nervous. She was not. She sniffed the back of my head, kissed my

husband's face and lay down on the back seat and went to sleep. She did not wake up until I pulled into our driveway. It was as if she knew she was going to her new home. When we got home she sat

patiently in the back seat and gave me time to open her door and grab her leash. She then

proceeded to calmly walk into the house and walked around as if she had always lived here and was

just returning from an outing. I showed her where the door to the yard was and where her dishes

were. She never had an accident in the house and from the start asked when she needed to go out.

    We had to show her that it was ok to sleep on the bed, the couch or any other piece of furniture.

We also had to teach her that her toys were hers. We showed her her toys and let her have them

whenever she wanted for as long as she wanted. There was only 1 time that she took something that

wasn't hers. My husband had a signed baseball sitting on top of our dresser. One day after Baby

had been playing with her balls she walked into the bedroom and came out with the signed ball. My

husband took it from her said no this isn't yours and then handed her one of her balls and said yes

this is yours. In the 5 years we've had her she's never again taken anything that wasn't given to her.

From the day we brought her home Baby has acted like she always lived here and always lived with us. She adjusted to everything easily and without any hesitation. She loves everyone that comes to the house unless they do something that she sees as a threat to us. She is a little wild when she greets someone but as soon as they acknowledge her with a pet she calms down and goes to lie down on the couch. Unless, she has recently been given a new toy. Then she has to run and get the new toy to show them. The visitor must tell her what a wonderful toy it is before she goes to the couch to lie down.

I've only had 2 experiences with Baby when she wasn't friendly with a stranger. Both times she thought she was protecting me. The 1st time was when I was taking her for a walk and my neighbor that she didn't yet know came walking over to me. He was calling to me in a loud voice and was holding something over his head. As he approached me she started snarling. He backed up, put what was in his hand down and then walked over to me talking softly. She was fine with him then.

The 2nd time was much scarier. My gardener came to the door to ask me something. I went out to

see what he wanted. As I usual I did I took Baby to the door with me but kept the glass outside door

closed and locked. The gardner had a leaf blower with him and was swinging the leaf blower back

and forth as he was talking to me. Baby saw the moving leaf blower, saw a man holding it that she

did not know and she dove through the glass door to chase him away. Thankfully she responds to

the command "get in the house" so once I gave that command she stopped chasing him so he didn't

get bit and she didn't get lost. Unfortunately, the glass had shattered when she went through it and

she got cut in several places. Off we went to the vet. I was a nervous wreck. She was perfectly calm

and went to sleep in the back of the car. Like the trouper she is she let the vet examine her and pull

pieces of glass out of her without any protest at all. Other than needing some stitches she was fine.

    About 6 months after we got Baby my husband had a stroke. Most dogs would have been freaked

out by strangers coming into the house and carrying their Daddy out. Baby looked at me, waited for me to tell her everything would be ok and went to her couch to rest. I of course left her and went to

the hospital with my husband. I was there for the next 16 hours. This poor dog was left alone in the

house after a traumatic incident. No dinner, no lights on because in my panic I had forgotten to put

lights on. When I returned home for a slight break she was still on the couch where I had left her.

For the next 2 weeks she adjusted to my routine of coming home early in the morning to let her out,

feed her and try to catch a few hours of sleep before going back to the hospital to be with my

husband. She was so good about this. This routine got a little better and I was able to leave the

hospital for more than a few hours so I started going home to sleep for the night. Again, she was my

comfort. Just as she had done when I was only home for a few hours she curled up next to me for

whatever time I tried to sleep and snuggled with me.

    When my husband was moved from the hospital to a rehab center the routine changed again.

First of all the visiting hours were much more limited so I was home with her much more. The bond we had starting from that first day I met her just kept getting stronger. After a few days at the rehab

center I found out that dogs were allowed to come visit as long as they stayed in a certain area

outside the facilities. Thus began another new experience for Baby. I would take Baby to the rehab

facility and wait for a friend to meet us there. The friend would then stay with Baby while I went inside

to get Jim. Again, I didn't know how she would react to being left with this friend in a strange place

and how she would react to the wheelchair my husband was in. As with everything else that has

been thrown at this resilient dog she took both of those things in stride. We did this several times a

week for many weeks while Jim was in rehab. Then he was transferred to a different rehab facility.

This one also allowed dogs to visit but they had a different routine. Dogs were allowed into the

building in the reception area and were also allowed into the courtyard. This meant a long walk from

the parking lot to the reception area of the rehab facility. It also meant many, many people would be

with her and around her, not just myself, Jim and my friend. Lastly instead of just having to deal with

1 wheelchair that my husband was in she was surrounded by strangers with, wheelchairs, walkers,

canes IV equipment etc. Again, she adjusted to all of it without a problem. She loved all the people

coming and petting her and making a fuss over her. She gave kisses to anyone that seemed to want

them. She walked past people having their lunch and never begged for food although if someone

asked me if they could give her something and I said yes she took it very happily.

Her ability to adapt to change was tested again when Jim came home from rehab. Thankfully, she

liked people so the horde of people that came through the house to make it accessible for Jim didn't

bother her. Neither did all the deliveries of special equipment for him to continue rehab at home.

Baby again took it all in stride. As long as I was ok with it so was she.

Jim came home and now there were strangers coming into the house all the time to help with

Jim's pt, ot and speech therapy as well as activities of daily living. She was a trouper through it all.

Eventually all that ended and things went pretty much back to normal. Baby settled in to being a dog

again. She keeps me happy with her joy in life and keeps me fit with her love of playing. She's back to being happy and carefree. She is mischievous and too smart for her own good. She opens doors

if they're not locked and follows me everywhere even when I don't want her to. She cannot be

allowed in the yard by herself because she will dig in the yard and try to get under or over the fence.

She insists on going out at least 10 times a day. All the things that she didn't do while we had to deal

with Jim's illness she does now. She has a very unique way of telling me that she's hungry; she goes

to her bag of kibble and sticks her nose in the bag. She in her own way has shown me how to adjust

to unforeseen changes in life and still find joy. She has been instrumental in helping me keep my

sanity and my perspective.

    And so the story continues. Every dog I've had has made my life better and has taught me life

lessons. The story will continue through all the dogs of my life.

Made in the USA
Middletown, DE
27 July 2024